GREAT PICTURES
AND THEIR STORIES

How To Look At Pictures

"You must look at pictures studiously, earnestly, honestly. It will take years before you come to a full appreciation of art; but when at last you have it, you will be possessed of the purest, loftiest and most ennobling pleasures that the civilized world can offer you."

JOHN C. VAN DYKE.

GREAT PICTURES AND THEIR STORIES

INTERPRETING MASTERPIECES TO CHILDREN

BY
KATHERINE MORRIS LESTER

BOOK SEVEN

ST. AUGUSTINE ACADEMY PRESS

This book was originally published in 1927
by Mentzer, Bush & Company.

This facsimile edition reprinted in 2024
with improved color images
by St. Augustine Academy Press.

ISBN: 978-1-64051-150-7

CONTENTS

INDEX OF ILLUSTRATIONS IN GREAT PICTURES AND THEIR STORIES

FOREWORD

Picture Study is rapidly becoming an important factor in our public school education. "Nearly every progressive city," says the Bureau of Education, Washington, D. C., "is making use of some form of picture study in the public school system."

The twentieth century has ushered in the reproduction of masterpieces in colors! To what heights of delight the children of the public schools may be carried by the famous pictures of the world in color!

It remains only for the elders to choose pictures adapted to the childish interests; pictures which will cultivate a taste for the best in art; pictures which through the impressionable early years will lead to a true understanding and appreciation of the world's masterpieces!

In preparing this series of readers it has been the aim of those selecting the pictures to consider always the child interest. The field of pictures is large. Not only have the "old masters" been drawn upon, but masters in modern art as well, including modern American artists. Thus constantly, through this series of pictures, the principles of beauty which made possible the "old masters" of yesterday are seen again in the art of today.

In the preparation of the text the child's interest and his ability to read are carefully considered. Real picture knowledge is conveyed in the child's own language.

In the primary grades the interest is largely in "what it is all about." Consequently the text aims to satisfy this curiosity, and at the same time lead to unconscious observation of those things which are most alive to the little child,—color, life, action.

The vocabulary for Books I, II, and III is based on "The Reading Vocabulary," * the Horn, Horn, and Packer List.

*See twenty-fourth Year Book, National Society for the Study of Education, Part I, 1925.

In the intermediate grades, a lively interest in the story is always uppermost. Gradually an appreciation of picture-pattern develops. Simple elements in picture making,—i.e. center of interest, repetition of line and color,—may be intelligently comprehended by children of the intermediate grades.

In the grammar grades great interest in the story continues, and with this interest there develops an appreciation of HOW the story is told,—the real ART of the picture. The pupil not only learns that the picture is a masterpiece, but WHY. He thus acquires standards for judging other pictures.

Each picture is followed by a short sketch of the artist, told in a key adapted to the age and interest of the pupil.

The questions which follow the text will assist in developing an intelligent appreciation of the picture.

The author is particularly indebted to Miss Jennie Long, recently Supervisor of Primary

Education, Peoria Public Schools, for valuable criticism of the primary text. Grateful acknowledgment is also made for the opportunity of practical work with a selected number of primary stories in the schools of Peoria.

The manuscripts of the intermediate and grammar grade books have been submitted to teachers of these grades, to whom the author is indebted for helpful practical suggestions.

The MUSICAL SELECTIONS for the pictures have been graciously contributed by Eva G. Kidder, Director of Music, Peoria Public Schools. The author believes this to be a very valuable feature of these books.

KATHERINE MORRIS LESTER.

ILLUSTRATED WITH REPRO-
DUCTIONS IN COLOR FROM
THE ORIGINAL MASTER-
PIECES, BY COURTESY OF
THE ART EXTENSION
SOCIETY OF NEW YORK.

MOONLIGHT, WOOD'S ISLAND LIGHT
Metropolitan Museum, New York

ARTIST: Winslow Homer
SCHOOL: American
DATES: 1836-1910

MOONLIGHT, WOOD'S ISLAND LIGHT

Over the lonely midnight sea
The silent moon hangs high;
A glowing moth with a trail of light,
It creeps across the sky.

A stretch of gray sea and night sky! The moon, veiled in mist and cloud, trailing a path of yellow light across the water! One lone wave breaking upon a rocky shore! Only the sound of the measured break disturbs the solitude. This is the silence of night.

It is the vastness of the sea under a night sky, silvered by moonlight, that the artist has transferred to canvas. Winslow Homer, the painter of the sea, looked out upon just such a scene as this. He placed it upon canvas exactly as it appeared. Once when asked if he ever changed or modified his color, he replied: "When I have selected the thing carefully, I paint it exactly as it appears."

In contemplating a picture such as this, we can well understand why artists find it difficult to paint pictures of the sea. In a vast expanse of water, whether quiet or in motion, there is little variety. This sameness of the sea gives the artist little opportunity to paint a picture worthy of his brush, unless, indeed, his own spirit is "one with the sea." And Winslow Homer's spirit was "one with the sea"! He has portrayed the sea in all its moods as no one else has ever done. He is America's greatest marine painter.

What a broad expanse of water! How gray and dark the sky! The big overturned wave in the foreground gives a note of cool blue to the gray of the sky and sea. The long path of yellow light murmurs a low receding harmony.

See how the water radiates the reflected light! Even the night becomes luminous. The very atmosphere becomes *colored air*! On the distant horizon, at the right, the lights of Wood Island dot the shoreline; the red glow of the lighthouse lamp throws its light over the scene.

Above hangs the moon in a softly diffused light. Its brightest light falls upon the hard sharp rocks in the foreground. The clear-cut contrast of greenish-black rock and the lighted areas, catches the attention and holds it here beside the overturned wave. Here the artist has concentrated both his color and light. Just beyond the wave, the lighted surface of the sea takes on more delicate tints. Gradually the light recedes. The path narrows. Slowly it trails off to the dim distant horizon.

How complete the picture! Nothing could be added, nothing taken away!

This completeness comes through the artist's understanding of design. His placing of the picture on canvas; his spacing of the various areas, sky, sea, and rocky coast; all has been carried out in just such a way that the whole becomes a unit of related spaces. Adding to this the note of color, he emphasizes and subordinates until he brings the parts together in one united whole.

So complete is the picture that it takes us entirely away from any thought of design, or pattern, or paint. We find our greatest pleasure in the loveliness of the scene before us. Such is the art of the great painter!

THE ARTIST

To live among the rocks high up above the sea; to hear the lashing foam cut the shore; to catch "the smell of the sea"; to enjoy its calm—this was the ideal life to Winslow Homer, America's painter of the sea. Solitary as a bird clinging to its mountain home, Winslow Homer kept his lonely studio high up on the rocky coast of Maine. Here he painted his pictures of the sea.

Homer was born in Boston, February 24, 1836. In the middle of the sixteenth century one of his ancestors crossed the Atlantic in his own ship. This was Captain John Homer. On his mother's side, too, there were sea captains. Homer himself claimed a pirate among his ancestors! So, you see the love of the sea was "in his blood"!

As a boy he attended school in Cambridge. Here he became known for his clever and rapid sketches. Among his playfellows his note-book of sketches was always of lively interest. Whether the lad had any serious intention of becoming a painter we do not know. We do know, however, that he was already an artist, whether he knew it or not. As he grew older his father advised him to become a salesman for a Cambridge merchant. The lad, however hesitated; he did not like the business world. He wanted to use a pencil and brush. He wanted to find his niche in the world!

One day his father read in a Boston paper: "Boy wanted. Apply to Buffer, lithographer. Must have a taste for drawing. No other need apply."

"Just the chance for Winslow"! exclaimed the father. "I shall go and see Buffer immediately!"

Fortunately Mr. Buffer was a friend of Mr. Homer's, and he very gladly agreed to take the boy on a two weeks' trial.

So Winslow went to work in the lithographer's shop. Here the work suited his tastes. He was employed in designing the title pages for music covers, and did other commercial work which came his way. Instead of remaining two weeks, he stayed two years.

Having made a success of this, he later set up a shop of his own. Here he took up the business of illustrating. Among the drawings of this period are those contributed to Harper's Weekly, which had been founded in the year 1858, a widely read magazine.

The next year found him in New York, still working away at his art. During the Civil War he was sent to the front as illustrator for Harper's Weekly. In 1862 he was with the Army of the Potomac. Every phase of camp life is illustrated in the drawings of this period.

It was after the war, in 1866, that Homer became enthusiastic in the use of water color. It was this year that he helped organize the American Water Color Society. In the medium of water color Winslow Homer is one of the greatest artists that ever lived. Many of his famous pictures in water color hang in the galleries of Chicago, New York, and Boston.

Though the artist became famous as "the painter of the sea," it was not until after he had returned from a visit to England in 1882, that he became a "dweller by the sea."

Then, going to the rugged coast of

Maine, he built his cottage high up upon the rocks, at Prout's Neck, near Scarboro. Here he continued to live and work.

From the window of his lofty workroom, he studied the sea in all its moods. Both the calm and the storm he knew by heart. During the day the lapping of the waves or the roar of the surf kept him company. At night the solitude of the sea breathed its benediction.

Homer knew not only the sea, but the sturdy fisher-folk who lived by the sea. He knew their work. He knew the rugged and hazardous life they led.

Many of the artist's earlier paintings picture this familiar side of the fisherman's life. "All's Well," "The Lifeline," "Undertow," "Fog Warning," are names which suggest the hardy life of those who live by the sea.

Later he omitted these sturdy figures, and painted only the mystery and grandeur of the sea. He painted the "might of the sea" as few others have done.

In order to adjust himself as comfortably as possible to the exact picture of the sea that he wanted, he built a portable cabin 8x10 feet, with a glass adjusted to one side. This he could plant on the rocks wherever he wished. Shutting himself within, he could paint undisturbed by the elements or by inquisitive intruders.

As his fame became widespread people were eager to know him. Many made pilgrimages to the Maine coast to see this man, who preferred above all else the companionship of the sea.

A gentleman who had become greatly interested in the painter and his work once traveled all the way from New York to Maine to make his acquaintance. Upon reaching the studio he found it empty. Greatly disappointed, he resolved to remain until he had accomplished the object of his journey,—to see and talk with Winslow Homer!

Leaving the vicinity of the cabin, he strolled along the shore. Soon he met a roughly clad old man carrying a fishing-pole.

"I will give you a quarter," said the stranger, "if you will tell me where to find Winslow Homer."

"Where's your quarter?" rejoined the fisherman.

The stranger passed over his quarter, and was astonished to hear the man say,—"I am Winslow Homer."

The story goes on to say that the artist took the visitor to his studio-home and there proved a right royal host.

America has come to look upon Homer as one of her painters who is distinctly American in every respect. He was untaught by foreign art, but developed his own thoroughly individual style. Moreover he found his subjects in the grandeur of his own New England coast.

STUDY FOR APPRECIATION

1. Who is America's greatest marine painter?
   Why is the sea a difficult subject?

2. Make a sketch of this picture showing the relation of sky, sea, and rocky coast.

3. Describe the effect of light on the atmosphere. On the sea.

4. Where has the artist placed his brightest light, strongest color, and sharpest accents? Why?

5. Name three ways in which the artist created distance.

6. What impresses you most in the picture?

Related Music: MOONLIGHT SONATA—
First Movement. *Beethoven*
MONDNACHT...*Schumann*

SIR GALAHAD
Private Collection

ARTIST: George Frederick Watts
SCHOOL: English
DATES: 1817-1904

SIR GALAHAD

Sir Galahad was the peerless knight of King Arthur's Round Table. He was the only knight destined to sit in the "Siege Perilous." This was a chosen seat at Arthur's great table. It was reserved for him only who should achieve the quest of the Holy Grail.

The Holy Grail, we are told, was the cup or dish used by Christ at the Last Supper. Joseph of Arimathea is said to have bought the cup from Pilate, and passed it on to his children, who regarded its care as a sacred trust. Later it was brought to England, where it was lost. It was believed to be hidden in an old castle, called "The Castle of the Grail." It was invisible to all save only to him who was perfectly pure in thought, word, and deed.

This mysterious cup bestowed miraculous favors on him who possessed it. It brought great wisdom, protection in battle, and constantly renewed life. There was one thing, however, which it did not do, it did not lessen the power of temptation. Even though a knight should possess the Grail, he could still be tempted. Consequently, though he be the perfect knight, though he possess the Grail, he must resist evil always.

The search for the Grail—"The Quest of the Holy Grail"—was undertaken by many of the knights of King Arthur's Round Table. It is said that some of the knights succeeded in obtaining a vision of the mystic cup, but none had yet possessed it.

Though this cup seems a material object, in the story it typifies all the ideals and aspirations toward which one strives. Just as the knights of the Middle Ages fared forth in quest of the Holy Grail, so today every youth, with his life before him, sets out with high hopes and noble ambitions.

As a youth Sir Galahad had served faithfully in preparation for knighthood. He had learned much about the exacting duties of knighthood. He had thought much of the Grail. Now he decides to set out on the adventurous journey. He recognized that the way would be difficult and perilous. As page and esquire, however, he had cultivated the virtues of courage and perseverence. These qualities were now a part of his character. He was, indeed, well equipped for any journey!

He wore the armour of a knight, and carried his shield and sword. There is a strange legend about Sir Galahad's shield and sword. The shield was found in an old, old church, where it had been left by one of his ancestors. Though it had lain here for centuries, it was visible to no one until Sir Galahad came.

His sword was found with the hilt projecting from a rock of granite. When the young knight placed his hand upon the hilt and drew upon it, lo, it yielded and came smoothly forth.

More strange than this, however, was the fact that, when he placed it in the scabbard which he carried, it fitted exactly. Still more strange were the words inscribed upon the sword. These words Sir Galahad read: "Never shall man take me hence, but only he by whose side I ought to hang, and he shall be the best knight in all the world."

Thus equipped, Sir Galahad set out upon his adventurous journey.

The story of Sir Galahad has inspired both poets and artists. George Frederick Watts, the English painter, composed our beautiful picture. He wanted to tell in color and form the story of the brave young knight as he journeyed in quest of the Grail.

He drew the youthful knight and the white horse so large that they almost fill the picture. Then he filled in the subordinate part of the canvas with landscape. Even this, however, helps to tell the story. The artist intended that every part of the picture should help to tell this most enchanting story.

See the protruding roots and trailing vines along the way! They impede the path. The way is uphill. Thus the artist suggests the obstacles and difficulties which obstruct the upward pathway toward the ideal.

The picture is largely dark, except for the bright light that falls upon the way. It lights up the face and armour of the knight. It lights up the whiteness of the steed.

The knight stands in silent meditation. One foot is upon the ascending path, suggesting that he goes forward. His face is thoughtful. His steady purpose and unfaltering courage are written in every line of the figure. He wears his coat of mail, and carries upon his shoulder his ancestral shield. His helmet is strapped to the saddle of his gentle steed.

See the fine white steed, his companion! He seems to understand all that Sir Galahad ponders. His intelligent eyes and erect ears suggest that he is alert and ready.

See the strong, arched neck! It tells of the great energy and physical strength needed in such a journey.

The fine figure of the knight and his snow white steed catch the full reflection of the distant light. The thoughtful face of the knight, framed in a mass of auburn hair, looks with calm determination toward the goal.

About Sir Galahad and his steed the artist has placed his accents of light and color. Here is red, the age-old symbol of loyalty, and white, the emblem of purity. These accents of light and color make this the "center of interest." By and by, however, we discover that other parts of the picture as well, the thick trees and the trailing vines, help to tell the full story of the "peerless knight."

Such is the figure of Sir Galahad! He it was, who with the other knights of the King Arthur's Round Table, took the most solemn pledge,—

"To reverence their king as if he were
  Their conscience, and their conscience as their
    king."

He it was who achieved the quest of the Holy Grail!

The artist, George Frederick Watts, suggests his idea of the young knight so vividly and so artistically that this painting is one of the favorite pictures of growing youth the world over.

THE ARTIST

This English painter, George Frederick Watts, was born in 1817. His parents were Welsh. The Welsh people are said to have a vivid imagination and a poetic temperament. Nearly all the many paintings of this artist reveal these gifts of imagination and poetic feeling. Watts painted two Sir

Galahads. One of them hangs upon the chapel wall of England's famous college, Eton; the original painting is in the private collection of Alexander Henderson, Esq., of London.

While a very small boy, Watts began to draw. It is said he began to draw as early as he began to talk. At a very early age he surprised his parents with the little drawings and original sketches he had made. As a child he was frequently found copying the quaint plates from an old, family prayer book. While still a youth, his original illustrations of the tales of Sir Walter Scott convinced his parents that the boy was highly talented. At fifteen he was painting in oils, and at twenty he was showing his pictures in the exhibitions of London. People liked his work. This greatly encouraged the young painter.

At twenty-five he entered a competition that brought him good fortune. A prize had been offered for the best design for a wall decoration for the new Houses of Parliament. Watts sent in a design, and to his great surprise received the first prize of £300. This was the turning point in his life. With the well-earned prize money he set out for Italy. His long cherished dream of studying in Italy was coming true!

In Italy he spent four years studying the works of the great Italian masters. Then he returned to England, where he worked out his new and original ideas.

During his long life of eighty-seven years he was recognized as one of England's greatest artists, and universally esteemed for his noble character and kindly spirit. Twice he was offered the honor of a baronetcy and as often declined, saying that such honors were unsuited to his "quiet tastes and moderate means."

As Watts grew older, he began to compose pictures that had a message. Some artists paint merely for the pleasure it gives them. Some paint landscapes, others portraits. Watts, however, painted with a moral motive, each picture must speak a message. In painting such a picture an artist continually draws upon his imagination. It was the vivid imagination of Mr. Watts that created many of his most famous pictures. Among them is our picture, Sir Galahad.

He was once asked about his style of painting. He replied: "I want to teach people how to live; how to make use of all their powers, to work, and hope, and enjoy life. Not merely to be slaves and drudges, but to care for something higher than money-getting and selfish pleasure."

In the painting of Sir Galahad he has this in mind. Above and beyond the story of the knight, "who knew not fear," is the spiritual message of brave and unswerving devotion to high ideals.

STUDY FOR APPRECIATION

1. Who was Sir Galahad?
   What period of history does he suggest?

2. What was his errand?

3. Describe his dress. His shield.
   Tell the story of his sword.

4. Explain why the artist chose a setting of thick woods and vines.
   Why is the step upward?
   Why is the light before him?

5. For what reason does the artist prefer a white horse?
   Is there any bond of friendship between the two?

6. Describe the colors and values that emphasize the "center of interest."
   Do the colors help in any way to tell the story? How?

7. Who is the artist?

Related Music: PROCESSION OF
                KNIGHTS—Parsifal...
                .... *Wagner*

THE VIGIL
Tate Gallery, London

ARTIST: John Pettie
SCHOOL: English
DATES: 1839-1893

THE VIGIL

In medieval times knighthood was the goal of ambition for every noble youth. As the honor was great, it was reserved for those tested and trained by a long course of arduous discipline.

After a youth had served to some king or knight as page or esquire; after his courage, loyalty, and gentle courtesy had been fully proven, he prepared for the long "watch" or "vigil."

The "vigil" was the all-night watch that preceded the ceremony conferring knighthood. It was the custom for those upon the threshold of knighthood to spend the night, before the eventful day, in prayer and devotion. The watch was kept, alone, before the altar of a Christian church.

In the painting, "The Vigil," the artist has pictured the interior of a great cathedral. Though we see only a small portion of it we know it must be lofty.

The artist, no doubt, wanted to suggest the vastness of the church and the height of the chapel, so he made the pillars great and massive.

It is night. The church is in darkness. The dim shadows lurk about the great columns. Somber and solemn is the silence. Only the kneeling figure of the knight in armour receives the full light. The reflected glow lights the pavement. This makes the darkness beyond the columns still more shadowy.

The candles are burning upon the altar. Though we cannot see them we know they are there. A portion of the figure of Christ upon the cross, the knight's inspiration to service, is plainly visible. Before the altar, in the full light, kneels the youth, consecrating himself, his sword, and his armour to the high ideals of chivalry. Before him lies his armour, his shield, and helmet. Clad in black, which suggests his readiness to meet death; a white tunic, typifying his purity of purpose; and a red mantle, a symbol of the blood he is prepared to shed, he spends the long night in prayer.

The youth clasps the unsheathed sword before him. He holds it firmly in a vertical position, most suggestive of strength. All the moral force of the knight is expressed in the clear cut line. Notice, also, that the erect figure of the knight repeats the same line of strength. The vertical edge of the white tunic, the line of the supporting column of the altar, and the distant pillars, all join in proclaiming this knight a man of great purpose and power. The artist chose these vertical lines because he knew they conveyed the impression of great strength.

Though the dark shadows and the height of the building suggest the solemnity of the occasion, the artist has added another note. Do you see the dark patches on the pavement? They are brasses, memorials to the dead buried there. It is here in the lonely church, among the tombs of the dead, that the vigil is kept. This is, indeed, a fitting close to the long years of preparation! It is, indeed, a fitting devotion for the exalted calling of knighthood!

The artist has composed his picture with the thought of emphasizing only the youth and the spirit of devotion. Consequently we do not notice much of the detail until we begin to study the picture-plan. Then we begin to see how all the details help to tell the story. We see, too, that the artist keeps all these details in a quiet light, subordinate to the beauty and impressiveness of the kneeling figure.

THE ARTIST

The youthful John Pettie was one of a group of four boys, who set out at a very early age declaring they were going to be artists. No one knew just how, or when, or where this was to come about. Each of the four, however, applied himself seriously to his studies. In turn success came to each.

Mr. Pettie was born in Edinburgh in 1834. He spent his boyhood in Scotland, where at sixteen he began his art studies. His uncle was a drawing master in Edinburgh, and it was under his direction that the lad received his first instruction.

Later he went to London. It was not long before he gained a footing as an artist of ability.

By and by, after his work had gained wide recognition, he was elected with full honors to the Royal Academy.

It is said that Mr. Pettie was gifted with a strong, wholesome, stimulating and refreshing personality. In his reading he was never contented with the ordinary stories. He delighted in books full of incident and exciting adventure. So keen was his pleasure in tales of contest and warfare, that his friends often remarked, in jest, that they found it necessary to restrain him from making his pictures "red with blood."

Mr. Pettie's pictures were largely historical. The days of chivalry and the old cavalier period furnished his imagination with vivid pictures. Moreover, he was a lover of costume. Costume, fitted to certain periods and occasions, was his delight.

He was a lover of color, and was as happy as a child in its use. In all of his pictures there is a fine harmony between the color and the mood or "spirit" of the painting. If the subject is sad or serious, the color is grave. If the subject is gay, the color sparkles. He painted "The Vigil" in 1884. In this picture is the same combination of appropriate color, fine design, and effective lighting that distinguishes all his works.

Though born in Scotland, Mr. Pettie lived most of his eventful life in London. Here he grew to fame. Today the larger number of his paintings hang in the English galleries. They are among the best historical paintings of our time.

STUDY FOR APPRECIATION

1. What does the word "vigil" mean?
   What was the vigil?
   Where was it kept?

2. How has the artist suggested the vastness of the church?

3. Where does the light fall? Why?

4. What is the character of the knight?
   How has the artist told this?
   Name the colors in the robes.
   What is the meaning of each color?

5. What takes place the following day?

6. Who is the artist?
   What kind of pictures did he paint?

Related Music: THE ROSARY ...... *Nevin*
CUJUS ANIMAM—Stabat
Mater .... *Rossini*

DANCE OF THE NYMPHS
Louvre, Paris

ARTIST: Jean Baptiste Corot
SCHOOL: French
DATES: 1796-1875

THE DANCE OF THE NYMPHS

A song without words! A poem of misty morning and coming light!

No artist ever painted the early misty morning as did Corot. What is it that makes his pictures different from all others? It is because Corot, who was highly sensitive to nature, felt that all about the trees, all about the streams, all about the hills and dales, was a very gentle spirit. This was the spirit of nature. Sometimes when he painted the trees, hill-sides, and misty distances he was able to put into them his own feeling about this spirit of nature. He did this in so effective a way that people always get the "feeling" of his pictures first. Then, because they, too, love this spirit of nature, they linger to study his paintings.

Corot's painting is not so much a painting of real trees, real distance and real figures, as it is his impression of the spirit of the morning. All about the landscape hovers this gentle spirit that he knew and loved so well.

See the soft feathery masses of rounded foliage against the morning sky! See the slender tree with the shimmering veil of delicate leaves! Under the arching foliage and through the open trees is a glimpse of the misty distance beyond. The sun will soon be up. Now it lights the sky. It turns the trees and their foliage to light yellow-green. It glints across the dew-covered carpet, making a pretty path of light for the frolicking nymphs.

These trees were personal friends to Corot. He painted them not as they really were, but as they appeared to him. Not a leaf is painted. All is one mass of light, delicate, quivering green, with cool hazy shadows. Notice how the artist carries the dark green of the willow out lighter and lighter, to the most delicate silvery tints. All about the leafy foliage, and through the broken masses lurks this spirit of nature.

See the beautiful curve of the big willow! See the gay curved line of the frolicsome nymphs below! Together they move in a rhythmic swing that makes the music of morning. With a soft, feathery curve the willow swings round. It droops and loses itself in the foliage of the smaller tree. Then, swinging up under the tree, the line of a graceful arch is formed. Here the arm of the dancing nymph takes up the curve and swings it out to her gay, glad companions. Then, on it goes to the merry young creature with up-raised arm at the left.

We scarcely catch this music of the swinging curves until we pause to study the picture pattern. We feel it, however, whether we know it or not, and this gives us joy in the painting. Corot's pictures are always in tones of pale greens, yellow-greens, gray browns, and gray. Occasionally the costumes of smaller figures, as in "The Dance of the Nymphs," enliven the scene with bits of bright color.

Before Corot's time there were very few painters of landscapes. It seems strange to us that the great out-of-doors did not attract the artists of an earlier day. Oh yes, trees were painted. Many artists of a hundred years before had painted trees. These artists, however, had not learned to study trees and landscapes out-of-doors. Trees grew, leaf upon leaf, upon their canvases. Each leaf was drawn and painted, making stiff little patterns of trees. These they painted in their studios, without so much as going out to study trees first hand. Later, in Corot's day, the painters set up their easels out-of-doors. They lived with the trees from misty morning till the moon came up. Thus they learned of the changing light and color. Since Corot's time the landscape painters of all the world study out-of-doors.

THE ARTIST

Corot was born in Paris over a hundred years ago. He was a little fellow with a long name,—Jean Baptiste Camille Corot. His father was a very prosperous shop-keeper, and was eager for his little son to grow up and become a business man. He placed him with a merchant in Paris, hoping he would develop a liking for trade. The little Camille, however, did not like shop and business. Every opportunity to get away from work found him with pencil and sketch book. His father finally despaired of a business career for his son, saying he would "never amount to anything." Though he was not happy to do so, he at length sent the lad to learn drawing and painting. When young Corot became older he went to Italy to study. His father was very kind. He provided him with money so he would have funds in case his pictures did not sell.

It was a long time before Corot's work attracted attention. His father naturally thought him a poor painter. One day while he was painting in Italy the well known director of the Academy of Rome passed him as he worked. Corot was practically unknown as an artist at this time. The trained eye of the director, however, recognized a fine quality in Corot's work. He stopped and examined his canvas, and congratulated the artist. The next day at the Academy he told his classes about the work of the young Frenchman. Not only did he praise the quality of his work, but he prophesied that Corot would some day be the master of them all.

Though Corot did not appear to place much confidence in the director's prophecy, he nevertheless enjoyed the reputation which it gave him among his fellow students.

Some years after, when he was about fifty years old the people began to realize that a great painter was in their midst.

People began to praise his style. They began to look for his pictures at the great exhibitions.

When his father heard about his son's success he could scarcely believe it. One day, meeting an artist who had studied with young Corot in Paris, he asked him if Camille *really* had any talent. "Tell me the truth," he said, "for you know what painting is." The artist found it difficult to convince the old man that his son was indeed "strongest" of all the painters of Paris.

Corot was very happy in his new found success. He worked hard, filling the many demands for his pictures.

It was his custom to rise about three o'clock in the morning. Going out to some favorite spot, he patiently waited until the morning advanced to the exact moment that pleased his fancy. Then it was that he began his sketches of the misty morning light.

Once upon a time he wrote:

"It is charming,—the day of the landscapist. One rises early, at three o'clock in the morning, before the sun shines. He does not see much at first; everything is scented, everything trembles with the first breeze of dawn. Bing! The sun is clear, though it has not yet torn away the mist behind which are hidden the hills of the horizon. Bing! Bing! The first ray of sun,— the second ray of sun. The little flowers seem to wake joyously. The leaves shiver in the morning breeze. In the trees the invisible birds are chirping. Bam! Bam! The sun has risen! Everything is brilliant! Everything is full of purple light!"

Corot's work brought him great wealth. This he gave liberally to poor struggling artists, and for the relief of the needy. In fact, he gave away his wealth in a prodigal fashion. His purse strings were always open. No one was turned away empty-handed. When those who were in need of money came to Corot, he would go to a table drawer, take out the needed amount, and pass it to the visitor without so much as a word.

Many of his friends remonstrated

with him. "Not at all," replied Corot; "it is my pleasure and my temperament. I can earn the money again so quickly, just by making a little branch. Charity always brings me more than it costs, for I can work better with a heart at ease. Once I gave away a thousand francs, a good deal for my little hoard just then, but the very next day I sold a picture for six thousand. You see it brought me a fortune; and that's the way it always is."

So little did Corot think about the business side of selling his pictures, that his friends again remonstrated with him. Finally he allowed them to set the price. "Very well," said he; "go yourselves and mark the prices on them." This they did; but Corot reserved the right to give away his pictures when it so pleased him.

His last pictures were painted for a great exhibition which was to be held in Paris in 1875. The pictures were completed; it only remained for the artist to add his name. Not being able to go to the studio, the pictures were brought to his bedside. After signing them, his thought seemed to wander to the lovely landscapes he had painted. Moving the brush back and forth as though painting, he exclaimed: "Look! How beautiful! I have never seen such lovely landscapes!"

These were his last words.

STUDY FOR APPRECIATION

1. Is this painting an "impression" or a "real" scene?
   How do you know?

2. What time of day is it?
   How do you know?
   Where is the sun?
   Trace the path of light about the picture.

3. Which are of greater importance, the trees or the nymphs?
   How do you know?

4. How has the artist simplified his landscape?
   Describe the pattern made by the trees against the sky.
5. Describe the colors in the picture.
   How many values of green do you see?
   What is the effect of the gradation of color in the sky?
6. Is there joy in the picture?
   Is there music in the picture?
   Where?
7. Who is the artist?
   What new manner of study did he introduce?
   When did he like best to paint?
8. How does Corot rank as a painter?
   Where is this picture?

Related Music: DANCE OF SYLPHS...
   ....*Berlioz*
   BALLET MUSIC FROM
    ROSAMUNDE..*Schubert*
   PIZZICATE FROM SYLVIA
    BALLET ....*Delibes*
   GAVOTTE—Mignon ....
   ....*Thomas*

ICEBOUND
Art Institute, Chicago

ARTIST: Willard Leroy Metcalf
SCHOOL: American
DATES: 1856-1925

ICEBOUND

Pictures are like people,—each has its peculiar character and charm. Nature paints beautiful pictures in every corner of the earth. Landscape is all about us. Spring, summer, autumn, winter, each has a beauty of its own. All that is necessary to make these changing pictures permanent is the artist—he who not only *sees* but possesses the gift of *making others see with him.*

In "Icebound" the artist caught the quiet charm of a winter scene with the bright sunlight reflected upon snow. It is a lonely spot, with whispering pines and faintly murmuring brook. Not a foot-print breaks the smooth surface of the snow! Nature alone, with Nature's children, the sky, the trees, the brook, keep tranquil company in this secluded spot.

How the white blanket shrouds the pretty bank! It makes the air cold and still. The pines whisper. The brook murmurs. It is winter.

The artist saw the beauty in this still, winter landscape. He saw the warm sun and the cool shadows. He saw the pretty pattern in the banks of the murmuring stream. He saw the cool green of the pines, and here and there patches of sunlight. He transferred this picture to canvas. We, too, may see the charm of winter in this secluded spot, just as the artist saw it.

See how the clear-cut line of the banks carries us back into the picture! We go to the far end of the brook. There the blue shadows, leading the way, take us up over the snow. Yes, over the snow we go, and back into the woods beyond! Then forward we come, down to the leafless pine at the right. The little blue line of shadow leads right down to the water's edge. Then up the brook, again we go! We could not go out of the picture if we tried. We stay within the big pattern just as the artist intended. He has arranged his pattern with this in mind.

In this scene the artist did not arrange his own composition. The composition was in the pretty scene before him. He, however, knew how to place it upon canvas to the very best advantage.

Do you know that snow is seldom white? Here it takes on the warm glow of the sun, with tints of rose. The blue shadows make a pretty lace-like pattern over the snow. They help to bring together the dark pattern of the trees above, and the light color of the banks below. These purple-blue shadows appear again and again in Metcalf's paintings. Someone has said that the artist "must have been born with a wood-violet before his eyes!"

See the solid mass of green above! How well the artist shows the kind of tree! The nearest trees catch the glow of the sun, turning them yellow-green. See the bright touches of light on the trunks! This gives life and sparkle to the mass of green. Through little openings in the trees we catch glimpses of the distant sky.

Notice how the artist has reflected the dark mass of green trees in the water. By adding light touches of foliage and shadow he suggests the movement of the brook. With the murmuring brook, the dark pines, and the sunlit snow, the artist has woven a pattern that unveils the mystery of Nature for those who have eyes to see.

THE ARTIST

It was not until Willard Leroy Metcalf was forty-seven years old that he became known as one of the foremost landscape painters of America. Though he had been drawing and painting ever since he was seventeen, it was not until the year 1903, at forty-seven, that life took a new turn. He calls this his "memorable year," and says his "new life," as an artist, dates from this time.

Mr. Metcalf was born in Lowell, Massachusetts, in 1858. He was seventeen when he began to study art in Boston. In the early days he worked as an apprentice in a wood engraver's shop in Boston, and gave his leisure time to the study of drawing. Here he learned one lesson that stayed with him always. He was taught "how to define the character of a tree in every detail through good draughtsmanship." In all of Metcalf's canvases his drawing of the character of trees is a distinguishing characteristic.

After several years of study both in America and Paris, he returned home and made the decision which changed his life.

He decided to take a year's leave of absence and paint nothing but landscape. He traveled to eastern Maine, and there he spent the entire twelve months in painting. At the end of that period he returned to New York. This was in 1904, the end of his "memorable year." He brought with him twenty-one canvases which he placed on exhibit. His success was immediate. From this time he became the Willard Leroy Metcalf whom we know as one of America's famous modern painters of landscape.

The most striking characteristic of Mr. Metcalf's work is the truthfulness of his pictures. He always caught the real likeness of the landscape, and then added to this, that something which is never seen but always felt, — the "spirit" of the place.

Unlike other artists of his day, he always kept his work smooth and even. This helps to give the air of serenity and mystery to his pictures.

His summer, autumn, and winter landscapes are remarkable in their fidelity to nature, and in the expert drawing of tree-character. They are bits of real scenery which he transferred to canvas, giving them the beauty and mystery which he felt.

STUDY FOR APPRECIATION.

1. What do you like best about this picture? Why?

2. What takes one into the picture? What keeps one within the pattern? Is this necessary to picture-planning? Why?

3. Describe the colors on the snow. Describe the trees and their colors. Describe the colors on the brook. What makes the water move?

4. Is this a real scene or an imaginative one? What is the "spirit" of a picture?

5. Who is the artist? For what is he especially known?

Related Music: WINTER CLOUDS.......
.... *Folk Song*

WINTER LONGING ....
.... *Peterson-Berger*

THE CONCERT
Berlin Gallery

ARTIST: Gerard Ter Borch
SCHOOL: Dutch
DATES: 1617-1681

THE CONCERT

Today, after nearly three hundred years, the beautiful pictures of the "little Dutchmen" are a delight to the whole world. These painters of Holland are often called "little Dutchmen," because at this time they formed a large group who were painting pretty little scenes of home life. Scenes indoors, and out-of-doors, and the common happenings of every day life, appealed to these painters of the Netherlands.

In this day there were no grand lords and ladies living in Holland. There was no court life to inspire the painters to large magnificent pictures. Their churches, too, made no demands upon them for religious paintings. So the artists of Holland contented themselves by painting beautiful little pictures of domestic life, pictures only large enough to hang upon the wall of the Hollander's simple home.

"The Concert" is one of the most famous of these little pictures. Perhaps the artist looked into this quiet room and saw the two girls playing their duet. It was just the kind of picture the "little Dutchmen" delighted in!

They liked to represent deep space as in a room. They liked to fill the space with softly lighted air. This made the objects in the room seem immersed in different degrees of shadowy light. They liked to illumine the principal figure with gay, bright color. This made the "center of interest" in the composition.

When the artist looked into this quiet room, the soft hazy light, and the gleaming satin dress captivated him.

The two girls are playing a duet. One plays the large bass viol, and the other the spinet. They are very quiet and serious. They are interested only in the beautiful harmony of the deep-toned viol and the sweet-toned spinet.

How subdued and soft is the shadowy light on the walls! The dark pictures seem veiled in the thin air. The chair, too, is soft and hazy. One figure sits facing us at the spinet. How tranquil and serene she is! The second sits with her back to us. But how charming she is! Her head with its mass of braided hair is a little inclined as she listens to the sound of the deep-toned viol. She wears the gleaming satin skirt that caught the artist's eye. Her satin jacket is of gay salmon-pink, with a fashionable collar of fur. Her skirt is spread out to the very best advantage. The light strikes full upon its gleaming folds.

How it illumines the satin sheen! How it sharpens the crisp edges! The magic in the artist's brush changes mere paint into satin!

Do you see the sharp oblique line of the skirt across the stool? Ah, yes, there is method here! This crisp oblique line is repeated again and again. First, the line of the arm, the scroll of the viol, and the collar repeat it; next, the lines of the spinet. These parallel oblique lines, one after the other, carry us back into the picture. This is the artist's way of leading back into the deep space of the room. The color becomes softer and softer as it leads from the brightest spot to the objects of less importance.

The white satin dress is a gleaming spot in the picture. It is repeated, in a softer light, in the neck of the girl, and again in the headdress of the quiet figure at the spinet. The beautiful color of the jacket is repeated, toned off, in the wood of the quaint little spinet.

See how the artist has placed his "darks"! From the dark collar of the playing girl the eye travels to the dark spots on the right wall, across to the picture on the left, then down the scroll of the viol, and back to the collar again. In this way the artist keeps the interest within the picture, never allowing it, for a moment, to wander outside.

We are not at all conscious of the plan of the artist. We know only that the picture is beautiful. However, when we begin to study the picture-plan, we discover that the artist has brought together lines, dark and light, and color, in so perfect a way that the result is a charming picture, a master-piece of art.

For nearly three hundred years "The Concert" has been considered one of the most beautiful of all the paintings of the "Little Dutchmen."

THE ARTIST

Gerard Ter Borch is said to have been the first of the Dutch painters to picture a satin gown. After his success it became the fashion among artists to dress their women in satin. It is also said that he originated the Dutch interior, which became so popular with the "Little Dutchmen."

This greatest of all the "Little Dutchmen" was born in 1617. His father was a well-to-do and well educated Dutchman. In his earlier days he had traveled extensively, visiting the great art centers of Germany, Italy, and France.

Though not distinguishing himself in any way, he found his greatest pleasure in painting, and in studying the old masters. Consequently when he discovered that his small son was showing talent for drawing, he was delighted.

The little Gerard's childish sketches of cows, and horses, old sheds, and thatched cottages greatly pleased his father. He kept all these little drawings. Frequently he made notes upon the margin. "Drawn by Gerard after nature on the 24th of April, 1626," is one notation. Another reads: "Made in 1625, on the 23rd of September, by G. T. Ter Borch the younger."

The elder Ter Borch was a wise father. He knew his son had great talent.

"Gerard must have a teacher!" he declared.

Forthwith he secured the best instructor to be had for the lad.

When Ter Borch grew older he entered the Guild of Painters at Haarlem, where he came under the influence of the famous Dutch painter, Frans Hals. Here he rapidly developed into a portrait painter.

The father was always interested in the progress of his son, and eager to assist him in every way. He sent him to foreign lands for travel and study. The young artist visited the large cities of Europe, studying the master-pieces of the greatest painters of the world. This was a rare privilege at that time, for traveling was less usual than it is today.

While in Germany, he happened to be in Munster when the famous peace treaty of 1648 was signed. Here he painted a large canvas showing all the dignitaries in attendance at the Congress. These were exact portraits, and so excellent in the rendering that they excited great interest and admiration. At once the artist became a favorite with the influential men at the Congress. The Spanish ambassador persuaded him to accompany him to Spain.

While in Spain he was received with great favor in court circles. He was invited to paint the king's portrait. This was a very distinguished honor. The king, in token of his appreciation, made him a chevalier, and presented him with his own royal portrait. The painter also received many gifts and honors from the Spanish people.

After many years of travel and study he returned to Holland to paint.

Just at the peak of his popularity William III, Prince of Orange, passed through the city where he was living. The towns-people, to do the prince full honor, requested his portrait as a gift to the city. Naturally they expected the great Ter Borch to be given the honor of painting the portrait.

The prince, however, was in no mood to sit for his picture, though he was not unmindful of the compliment.

Upon returning home he sent these worthy Hollanders a portrait of himself painted by a popular French artist of that day.

The magistrates of the town met in solemn council. Very respectfully they declined the gift, not, however, without reminding the prince that their fellow citizen, the great Ter Borch, was worthy to be the master of the French painter.

It is said that, by and by, the prince consented to sit for Ter Borch, and that this famous Dutch master painted his portrait several times.

During the time of his popularity, Holland was enjoying great prosperity. The homes of the well-to-do citizens were being adorned with beautiful furniture. The dress of both men and women was taking on the line and color of fashion.

Ter Borch was still at the height of his power. He soon became the painter of the fashionable circles of Dutch society. The interiors of beautiful homes, women in shimmering satin, and men in elegant attire, made constant demands on his time and talent. Before long his reputation became widespread, and his works were being engraved by the best craftsmen in the country.

As a painter of this period in Dutch life he is without a peer. Others have pictured Dutch life. Others have attained fame. None, however, have surpassed Gerard Ter Borch in that air of elegance that distinguishes all his paintings. He is often called "the painter of fashion." His little pictures are "precious documents" portraying the life of that distant day.

STUDY FOR APPRECIATION

1. Why did the Dutch artists paint interiors?
   How did they fill the room space?
2. Where is this pretty interior?
   What are the girls doing?
   Name the instruments?
3. Describe the position of the foremost girl. Of the far figure.
   Of what period are the costumes?
4. What is the "center of interest?"
   How has the artist directed attention here?
5. Describe the most illumined color.
   How do the colors recede?
   What effect does this have?
6. How has the artist arranged his "dark"?
   What effect does this have?
7. Who is the artist?
   What did he originate?
   To what group does he belong?

Related Music: THE SWAN....*Saint Saens*
SLUMBER SONG...*Popper*

KING COPHETUA AND THE BEGGAR MAID
Tate Gallery, London

ARTIST: Sir Edward Burne-Jones
SCHOOL: English
DATES: 1833-1873

KING COPHETUA AND THE BEGGAR-MAID

The story of the African king, Cophetua, who married the "beggar in gray," and made her his queen, is one of the oldest in the English language. It is often alluded to by Shakespeare, Ben Jonson, and other English poets and dramatists.

One day this African king, so the story runs, looked out from his palace window and there below espied a group of beggars. Down he went to the palace gate. Immediately the beggars raised their voices in a cry for alms:

> "The Gods preserve your majesty,
> The beggars all gan cry:
> Vouchsafe to give your charity,
> Our children's food to buy."

The king threw his purse among them. Hurriedly they divided the contents and moved on. One only, the "beggar in gray," tarried.

"The king he cal'd her back againe,
　And unto her he gave his chaine;
And said, With us you shall remaine
　Till such time as we dye:
For thou, quoth he, shalt be my wife,
　And honored for my queene;
With thee I meane to lead my life,
　As shortly shall be seene;
Our wedding shall appointed be,
And everything in its degree:
Come on, quoth he, and follow me.

　　．　　．　　．　　．　　．　　．　　．

Thus hand in hand along they walke
　Unto the king's pallace:
The king with courteously comly talke
　This begger doth imbrace:
The begger blusheth scarlet red,
And straight againe as pale as lead,
But not a word at all she said,
　She was in such amaze.
At last she spake with trembling voyce,
And said, O king, I doe rejoyce
That you will take me for your choyce
　And my degree's so base."*

The story of King Cophetua and the
beggar maid has inspired many artists,
but none has approached Sir Edward
Burne-Jones in the artistic interpreta-
tion of the story.

Burne-Jones first of all is a designer.
Beauty of design places this painting
first among his many masterpieces.

---

*Reliques of Ancient English Poetry, Thomas Percy,
Bishop of Dunmore.

Here the beggar maid, still "in gray," is seated on the king's throne. The king has relinquished his seat, and sits below on the steps of the dais. He wears gleaming black armour. His dark head is clearly outlined against the background. Upon his knee he holds a beautiful crown of jewel-like metal studded with rubies.

The throne with its settings suggests all the sumptuousness of the Orient. The panels of chased gold gleam with a soft mellow light. The hangings are the richest of fabrics from the East. Luxurious cushions lie upon the throne seat. Above, two standing figures, gazing down upon the scene, chant a low sweet melody. Beyond, through the open window, is a glimpse of distant landscape.

Such is the setting of the story.

Through his understanding of design the artist has arranged a beautiful pattern of dark and light, color and line.

See the strong vertical lines of the setting! They conform to the general shape of the panel. The artist has constantly repeated the same vertical movement within the design itself. First, the panels of the throne give force to the upward movement. Again, the standing figures above reinforce the same movement. Even the fall of the curtains and hangings repeats this scheme of the general design.

The vertical movement of the pattern is broken by a few subdued horizontal notes, the steps, the seat, the upper line of the paneling, and the support of the blue curtains.

In the midst of this beautiful setting, and giving accent to the pattern, sits "the begger in gray." The artist has posed the figure in such a way that the feet are drawn back. This pose gives an accented diagonal line of light from the knee to the feet. It helps to carry the eye down to the lower part of the pattern. Notice that this same line is repeated, reversed, in the line leading from the knee of the king to his feet, drawn back, upon the lower step.

Burne-Jones was a designer in color as well as in line. See the "darks" and "lights"! See the arrangement and placing of the rich tones of color! The beggar maid, herself, by the contrast of dark and light and placing, dominates the scene. The dark knight, in still darker armour, and the dark notes of the shield and standard, opposite, frame in the setting. The eye, following the lead of the steps, is carried into the picture between the two dark notes, the king and the standard opposite; then passes beyond to the beggar maid, the queen upon her throne. All other color in the design is subordinated to these strong notes. The rich grayed tones of yellow, red, and blue melt together forming a tapestry-like background, against which the figure of the beggar maid is relieved.

There, timid and half afraid, she sits

motionless. The king, too, upon the steps below, is absorbed in his own thought.

> "And when the wedding day was come,
>   The king commanded strait
> The noblemen both all and some
>   Upon the queene to wait.
> And she behaved herself that day,
> As if she had never walked the way:
> She had forgot her gown of gray,
>   Which she did weare of late.
> .   .   .   .   .   .
> And thus they led a quiet life
>   During their princely raigne;
> .   .   .   .   .   .
> Their fame did sound so passingly
> That it did pierce the starry sky,
> And throughout all the world did flye
>   To every prince's realme."

Every detail of the picture is wrought with the greatest care. The armour and shield of the king are exquisitely drawn and painted. It is said they were especially prepared for this picture after designs by the artist. The panels of the throne, as well, were prepared with beaten gold.

When one contemplates the beauty of design and the jewel-like surface of this picture, he is reminded of the words of the artist:

"I love to treat my pictures as a goldsmith does his jewels. I should like every inch of surface to be so fine that if all but a scrap from them were burned or lost, the men who find it might say, 'Whatever this may have represented, it is a work of art, beautiful in surface, and quality and color'."

THE ARTIST

Sir Edward Burne-Jones was born in 1833, in the large manufacturing town of Birmingham, England. It was a busy city of factory workers. There was little in it to interest this dreamer-boy, unless it was the many books in the shop windows. He used to stand outside gazing in upon them, wondering about the stories they might contain, and wishing he might read them.

One day a relative sent him a copy of *Æsop's Fables*, and from that day on his life grew very much brighter.

The boy's father had made plans for him to become a clergyman, and later sent him to Oxford University. There he met many students who, like himself, were interested in art. This seemed to be the world he had been trying to find, a world in which he could picture his visions.

He soon decided to become a painter, and journeyed to London, where he began his studies in art. He was a grown man when he took his first lessons in drawing. He was, however, so earnest in his desire and so faithful in his work, that he did not go unnoticed.

His teacher marveled at his genius, especially in designing. When Burne-Jones found it difficult to pay for his lessons, his teacher turned work which came to him over to his gifted pupil. While working here with this teacher Burne-Jones made designs for stained-glass windows. They were so beautiful that they brought wide-spread attention to the artist. Later he became famous for his beautiful designs for windows. In our own country the people of Boston point with pride to a fine window in Trinity Church of that city, as a "Burne-Jones window."

He continued to study and work here with his teacher. More and more people began to discuss his art. The papers had much to say.

At first people did not like his fanciful ideas. They did not understand these strange figures of his imagination, and the scenes in which he placed them.

Criticism and ridicule were heaped upon him. The papers of the day came out with such witticisms as,—"Burn Jones! Burn Jones!"

But Burne-Jones kept right on. One day England forgot her criticism, forgot her ridicule, and heaped favors upon this poet-artist whom they had just begun to understand.

Burne-Jones had come into his own! Though personally he cared little for wealth or fame, all England acclaimed his genius and bestowed upon him both riches and honor. In recognition of the high esteem in which he was held by the English nation, Queen Victoria conferred upon him the title of baronet. Since that time he has been known as "Sir" Edward Burne-Jones.

The work of Burne-Jones is distinctly different from that of any other artist. His pictures are patterns of beauty worked out in his own imagination. No one ever saw human beings such as Burne-Jones paints. They are all delicate poetic fancies of his own mind. He never painted landscapes. The world without had no charms for him. It was always to the old myths and fairy tales that he turned for inspiration. Then about these fair creatures of fancy he wove his patterns of line and color in which all the world has since rejoiced.

STUDY FOR APPRECIATION

1. What is the story of King Cophetua and the Beggar Maid?

2. In what form has the artist told his story?
   What is the dominant movement of the panel? How is it varied?

3. Where are the darkest notes in the picture?
   Why are they placed as they are?

4. How is the eye led into the picture?
   What carries the eye to the upper part of the panel?

5. What is the "center of interest"?
   How has the artist directed attention here?

6. Who is the artist?
   For what is he especially noted?
   What great honor was conferred upon him?

Suggested Musical Selection:
        SALUT D'AMOUR (Love's Greeting)
    .... *Elgar*

MICAH, HAGGAI, MALACHI, ZECHARIAH
Boston Public Library

ARTIST: John Singer Sargent
SCHOOL: American
DATES: 1856-1925

MICAH, HAGGAI, MALACHI, ZECHARIAH

From the Frieze of the Prophets

Here stand four impressive figures. Each is a prophet of old. Three catch the vision of a brighter day; one, in despair, turns away.

Haggai, Malachi, and Zechariah are prophets of hope, but Micah cannot see the vision of a coming light.

This panel is one of a series of five which forms a beautiful wall decoration in the Boston Public Library. This celebrated series of five panels is known as the "Frieze of the Prophets." It occupies the width of the wall space above the door at one end of the long corridor known as Sargent Hall. This corridor is named in honor of the American artist, John Singer Sargent, who planned and executed the decoration.

The "Frieze of the Prophets" is only a part of an elaborate scheme of decoration in Sargent Hall. It is, however, so completely a unit in itself, that it alone has become justly famous.

The complete plan of decoration pictures the triumph of Christianity. The "Frieze of the Prophets" suggests the great religious ideas and ideals from which Christianity developed. True religion is based on the worship of one God rather than many gods, and true worship recognizes the Law and the Prophets.

These prophets of the Old Testament were an unusual group of men. They had much to do with the history of the ancient world as recorded in the Bible. They were men of character, and deeply religious. They seemed to be directly inspired by Jehovah, and spoke without fear. They constantly warned the people to turn from their many idols to the worship of the one true God. They found their work most difficult. Many of them despaired. Others were hopeful.

The great religious leader of the Hebrews was Moses,—he who brought the commandments down from Sinai. He was the founder of the Jewish nation, and of their religion. Some one has said: "Amongst all lawgivers, founders of states, and teachers of mankind, none has equaled Moses." He was destined to lead the people from the worship of idols to the service of the one true God.

With Moses the Lawgiver as the center of the frieze, the artist has arranged the prophets on either side. Nine form at the right, nine at the left, making in all nineteen majestic figures. Those standing at the right of Moses are Elijah, Daniel, Ezekiel, Nahum, Amos; those at the left, Joshua, Jeremiah, Jonah, Isaiah, Habakuk, Micah, Haggai, Malachi, and Zechariah.

Our picture represents the last panel to the left of the central figure. Here stand Haggai, Malachi, and Zechariah, with the one despairing note, Micah.

Though Micah bows his head upon his hand in deep grief, he is still a man of strength, as suggested by the long straight edge of his mantle.

The three figures, Haggai, Malachi, and Zechariah, are men of vision. They see far beyond their troubled time and the idolatrous worship of their day. Their fine faces, deep set eyes, and upraised arms carry the thought up, out, and forward to the time toward which they point. That time is the age proclaimed by the prophets of the Old Testament. It is the time to which the New Testament bears witness. They point to the coming of a Messiah. In the Messiah they see one who will redeem the world. They see the service of idols forgotten in the new understanding and worship of the *one true God.*

Notice the composition of the group. He who is downcast turns his head away. Thus he withdraws in thought from the others. His face is shadowed.

The three of the same hope, of the same vision, move together, heads up, buoyant, free. The light falls full upon their upturned faces! Notice the varying shades of expression and feeling. The face of Zechariah is almost ecstatic as he looks into the future.

See the pattern of light and dark made by the simple masses of drapery! Each figure is enveloped in a great mantle. Each mantle hangs in large unbroken folds to the feet. This simplicity of surface serves to emphasize the heads of the prophets, and to bring their expressive faces into full relief. Occasionally the long vertical edge of a scarf or fold gives variety to these simple surfaces, thus adding the vertical note of stability, and investing the character of these historic figures with strength and majesty.

The long straight edge of Micah's mantle is sharply silhouetted against the dark of his robe. This is repeated in the accented edges of Haggai's enveloping mantle, and the line of the up-raised arm. Again it is repeated in the straight edge of white against the brown mass of Malachi's robe. The same line is repeated in the hanging end of Malachi's scarf, and the sleeve sharply silhouetted against the white robe of Zechariah.

So it is with the entire panel of five. Each group is complete in itself, and yet by the direction of line, position of figures, and pattern of light and dark, the entire series is bound together as one.

Like a human wall, with our panel a part of that wall, stand these giants of old. Their backs are turned forever upon the idolatrous past, and they look forward with an unconquerable faith to the time when all peoples shall know and worship the one true God.

It is said that the artist, before attempting to design this great decoration, spent many years in studying the Bible. The lives of the prophets, their hopes, their ambitions, their victories and their disappointments, were of absorbing interest to him.

So complete was Mr. Sargent's understanding of the character of each of the prophets that he was able to give it expression in his decoration. Through line and color, in the form of design, he has told the life-story of each prophet quite as completely as another might write it in words.

THE ARTIST

It was in the beauty-loving city Florence, Italy, in 1856, that John Singer Sargent was born. Here with his American parents, living in a beautiful home in the suburbs of Florence, the lad passed his boyhood. It is said that the boy's mother, though making no claims to artistic talent, possessed ability for drawing and painting. No doubt the youthful Sargent inherited this gift, which later was developed and stimulated in the artistic atmosphere of his birthplace.

As a boy he roamed at will among the famous picture galleries of Florence. Occasionally he traveled to Paris and the French coast.

A pretty story is told about the young lad's first box of colors. One day he sat on the seashore sketching a picture of the sea. While he was working a lady passed by. She paused to watch the youthful artist. Becoming more interested, she ventured to offer a word.

"Why do you not paint your picture with colors?" she asked.

"Because I haven't any," replied the boy.

With a word or two more she passed on. Shortly, however, she returned, and presented the lad with a box of colors. This is said to have been the first box of colors used by the now famous painter, John Singer Sargent.

It was in the city of his birth, however, the beautiful city of Florence, that Sargent received the inspiration which later led him to the very heights of his profession.

After studying at the Academy of Florence, where he received instruction in drawing and painting, we find him at the age of nineteen setting out for Paris. He carried with him a portfolio of drawings which he hoped to offer as samples of his work, and evidence of his sincerity of purpose. Arriving at the French capital, he presented himself at the studio of one of the distinguished masters of the day. Impressed with the young man's work and his pleasing personality, the artist accepted him as a student.

Working tirelessly in the studio day by day, young Sargent soon surpassed his master. He put endless effort into all his work, never attempting to arrive by a "short cut." He was capable of "infinite pains." Leaving Paris he later traveled extensively, studying the great old masters of the past. By the time he was thirty-three he had gained real distinction in both Europe and America.

As a portrait painter, John Singer Sargent ranks unquestionably first. His celebrated portraits of notable men and women alone would place him foremost among American artists. It has been said: "To have been painted by Sargent added distinction to the distinguished."

Though Mr. Sargent's portraits place him in the first rank, he is also justly celebrated as a water colorist and mural painter. His decorations in the Boston Public Library have been likened in originality and power to the world-famous frescoes of Michaelangelo and Raphael.

As with many of the truly great, Sargent was of a modest and kindly temper, beloved by all who knew him.

At the time of his death in 1925 he was said to be "the greatest figure in nineteenth and twentieth century art."

STUDY FOR APPRECIATION

1. Name the prophets of this panel.
   Who are the prophets of hope?
   Why?
   Who is the despairing prophet?
2. How has the artist expressed hope?
   How has he expressed despair?
3. How do these men impress you?
   Does their position help to create this impression? How?
   Does their dress help? How?
   Do the lines of the composition help? How?
4. What is the general subject of the decoration?
5. Where is this panel placed in the frieze?
6. What was the message of the prophets?
   What was the vision they beheld?
7. Who is the artist?
   For what is he especially noted?

Related Music: THE PROPHECY—Coming of the King........*D. Buck*

BARTOLOMMEO COLLEONI
Venice, Italy

ARTIST: Andrea del Verrocchio
SCHOOL: Italian
DATES: 1435-1488

BARTOLOMMEO COLLEONI

Who is this rider, stern of countenance, with deep-set eyes and an iron will! Who is this warrior bold!

About five hundred years ago a poor unknown young man, without occupation, offered himself to the officers of the Venetian army. This young man was Bartolommeo Colleoni.

In the army he soon attracted the attention of his superior officers. Before long he was himself made an officer. He proved so able that he quickly rose to greater prominence. As general, he became the friend of princes. Later he was promoted to the highest military post in the Venetian Republic. He became General-in-Chief of the Venetian armies.

Colleoni was every inch a soldier. Constant exercise kept him fit. It is said that wearing his armour, he could outrun the swiftest in his camp. Without his armour, few, indeed, were even the horses that could outstrip him.

Though he was a soldier, he loved study and the society of scholars. He made his camp a gathering place for students and men of affairs. History says that he was a good man, a just man, and that he dealt kindly with his people. This is saying much, for in that period of Italian history there was much of cruelty, bloodshed, and crime.

When Colleoni died, it was found that his fortune had been left to the Venetian Republic,—on one condition. A statue must be erected to him in the great square of St. Mark!

It was, however, against the law to place a statue in this great square. Finally it was decided to place the statue in another square, also a Square of St. Mark, but much smaller and removed some distance from the center of the city.

Today, in the little Square of St. Mark, stands the Colleoni,—the greatest equestrian statue in the world!

Here it has stood for nearly five hundred years. Never before had an artist attempted a prancing steed! Colleoni's statue was different from all others. Here the artist lifted the foreleg of the horse as if he were moving forward. He suddenly becomes alive! He becomes a wonderful steed,—full of fire, full of pride, full of power.

And what shall we say of the rider? A Colleoni of iron! A Colleoni whose glance never quailed before the foe!

He sits in complete armour, drawing himself up to the fullest height. His head is turned, as he looks out defiantly. Horse and rider are one in their haughty pride. They move together in spirit, feeling, and form.

Notice the delicate design worked out on the saddle and trappings. This hints of the artist's training as a goldsmith. Do not let the knotted mane escape you! So marvelous a creation as the Colleoni deserves all the praise it has received through the centuries.

THE ARTIST

Andrea del Verrocchio was born in 1435. Though he is known as one of the greatest sculptors of the fifteenth century, he was as well a designer, a goldsmith, and a painter.

Verrocchio enjoyed a wide reputation as a painter, but one day he ceased to paint and turned his attention to sculpture.

Among the pupils in Andrea's studio was a handsome lad with flowing curls, who usually wore a rose-colored coat and long hose. This was the youthful Leonardo da Vinci.

One day while Verrocchio was working on a large picture, he fell ill. Unable to paint, he selected the most capable of his pupils to complete the work. This was the young Leonardo.

"Do thy best," said the master to the youth, as he turned away, too ill to give him any supervision.

The youthful Leonardo realized the

serious responsibility which had fallen upon him. With hesitating hand he took the brush, then knelt and said a prayer: "It is for my beloved master; I implore skill and power for this deed."

The work was later completed.

Verrocchio was led by his pupils to the studio to view the picture. He sat before it. Leonardo, kneeling beside him, waited. The teacher looked in silence. Not a word was spoken. At last Leonardo spoke. "Master," said he. Verrocchio threw his arms around him, and burst into tears.

"My son," said he, "I paint no more; to thee I commit my pencil and palette."

From that time Verrocchio painted no more. Leonardo became the pride of his life. This same Leonardo grew to be one of the greatest Italian masters.

Now Verrocchio gave his attention to sculpture. He attracted the attention of the most powerful princes of

Italy. Then it was that, next to discovering Leonardo, the greatest event in his life happened. He was commissioned to model the great Colleoni!

With great care and study he modeled the horse. Soon he heard that another artist had been chosen to model the figure of Colleoni. So angry did he become, that, in a fit of temper, he broke the legs and head of the horse.

When the rulers of Venice heard this, they were highly indignant. They sent word warning the artist never again to appear in Venice, under penalty of being beheaded. The artist was not disturbed. He sent back word saying: "You must not cut off my head, for you can never replace it; while I can easily replace the head and legs of the horse."

The fearlessness of the reply impressed the rulers. They begged him to return. They promised double pay. They assured him they would never again interfere with his work.

Verrocchio returned to Venice. His work completely absorbed him. At last the great Colleoni was finished!

STUDY FOR APPRECIATION

1. What name is given a statue of horse and rider?

2. Who is this rider?
   What qualities do you read in his figure?

3. What is the feeling common to horse and rider? Why do you think so?
   What effect does this have on the general design?

4. What new experiment did the artist make in modeling this statue?

5. Who is the artist? When did he live?
   Relate his experience while modeling the "Colleoni."

Related Music: WARRIOR BOLD...*Adams*
LO! THE CONQUERING
HERO COMES!..*Handel*

AVENUE MIDDLEHARNIS
National Gallery, London

ARTIST: Meindert Hubbema
SCHOOL: Dutch
DATES: 1636-1709

AVENUE MIDDLEHARNIS

This old world of ours has always had its hills, rivers, skies, and sunshine. It is difficult to believe that artists have not *always* painted landscape. But the story of painting tells us that the pictures of the great out-of-doors did not come until long after other subjects had been painted for many, many years. Oh, yes, trees, mountains, and rivers were painted, but they were not real mountains, real trees, or real rivers. Stiff little patterns of trees decorated the early pictures. A curved line represented a mountain; a zig-zag line, a river.

These early painters of outdoor scenery never intended their pictures for landscape, as we understand it today. They were painted only as backgrounds for the *real* picture. The *real* picture was usually a figure or a group of figures. Indeed, figures were of first importance in these early landscapes, for artists recognized no beauty in anything aside from human life. There were no mountains, trees, sunlight, no shadow, no perspective.

This picture of the old roadway in Holland, Avenue Middleharnis, is one of the famous early paintings of landscape. Here are real clouds! Here is real sunlight! Here is true perspective.

It is about two hundred years ago that this picture was painted by the Dutch master, Meindert Hobbema. Strange to say, it attracted no attention whatever. People were not interested in pictures that showed the real country with which they were already familiar. So the great artist died poor and unknown. However, by the time the greater part of a century had rolled away, the world had wakened up. Now he was recognized as among the greatest of the early Dutch painters. Today not only Holland, but all the world honors Meindert Hobbema.

Hobbema had probably walked along this road many times. He had made many observations for himself. He made a mental note of the great expanse of sky, and the beautiful, moving, cloud forms patterned against it. He watched the sunlight as it peeped now and then from behind the clouds, and lighted the landscape. He noted the tall poplars that bordered the road. He observed their slim lines and bushy tops. He studied them as they marched in rhythmic measure to the far distant village, and there disappeared. All these things he observed and stored in his mind to use later.

See the great expanse of sky! It covers more than two thirds the canvas. Against it are cloud forms as real as any that ever floated in a Holland sky! See the pattern they make against the background.

The two stately poplars rise in the foreground. They stand tall and straight. They are first in the long line that moves back, and back, toward the horizon. See the perfect perspective! The near trees are tall and spaced far apart, but as the line recedes they become smaller and smaller, closer and closer, until they disappear on the edge of the village.

Middleharnis borders on the North Sea. There in the distance rises the tall spire of the Town church. Round about are the red roofs of the village.

How the old roadway widens as it comes down toward the front of the picture! A hunter with his dog walks along the road. How small he seems beside the tall trees! Hobbema, you see, is painting landscape for itself, and not as a background for figures, as did the early painters.

On each side of the road are the familiar ditches for irrigating the land. In the center foreground a cross-road leads to right and left. On one side is a nursery garden with its tall trees and shrubs. Here stands the sturdy Dutch gardener, pruning his trees. On the other side is a group of green trees.

It is a quiet scene. Nothing disturbs the serenity of this Holland landscape. The artist has not permitted any diagonal lines, of consequence, to creep into his picture. His accents are of the tall verticals and the long horizontals. Each is constantly repeated in the picture. The tall poplars are repeated in the church spire, the shrubs of the nursery garden, the trees at the left. The long line of the horizon is repeated in the cloud forms, the cross-road, and other minor accents of "dark" and "light." This is the secret of the quiet and repose of the landscape.

The long avenue fills the very center of the picture. All else is merely the setting. But how well balanced the picture! How superb the "center of interest"! It is the Avenue Middleharnis with the receding lines of the tall poplars that Hobbema has made immortal!

THE ARTIST

Meindert Hobbema is one of the great names in Dutch art. Like many of his countrymen he, too, was poor and unknown during his lifetime. It took the world about one hundred years to reach the place where it could understand and appreciate the pictures which he painted. Even then it was not his own country, Holland, but England that first recognized his genius. Consequently many of his pictures are owned in London.

Hobbema was born in Amsterdam in 1638. Though we know very little about him, the records of Amsterdam show that he was a pupil of the famous painter, Jacob Ruysdael, who painted "The Mill." Though he and Ruysdael lived and painted at the same time in Amsterdam, their work is very different. Hobbema painted the landscape as it was. Ruysdael put more of his own "feeling" into his pictures. He seems to have had more imagination than Hobbema. Like Ruysdael, Hobbema could not draw figures to his satisfaction. Consequently other artists were usually called into the studio to add the necessary figures in a landscape.

Hobbema was a lover of nature as he found it. He did not seek for unusual or ideal scenes to paint, but painted the landscape as he saw it. While some artists prefer twilight scenes where everything is seen through a soft veil, or the brilliant sunsets, where all is aglow, Hobbema selected those in full daylight with the sun shining through the trees. Such pictures of Holland breathe a spirit of contentment and peace.

It is said that Hobbema's paintings brought him scarcely anything. He probably gave many of them away. He did not paint for wealth, but only because he loved to paint. It is said that he painted only "when the spirit moved him." From 1670 until 1709, the year of his death, he painted only one picture, and that was the famous "Avenue Middleharnis," which he signed and dated.

Though he painted few pictures, it is said that their sales a century later would have made him the wealthiest man in Holland. And yet, poor Hobbema was so neglected during his lifetime! His last days were spent in the almshouse of his native land.

It has been about two hundred years since this great painter left the world. What a change has come! Today his pictures hang in the great galleries of England, Berlin, Brussels, and Amsterdam. Beautiful reproductions of many of these originals have been made. The reproduction of his masterpiece, "Avenue Middleharnis," hangs in many schools, colleges, and public buildings in many parts of the world.

Today this picture is ranked among the greatest of early Dutch paintings. We, of the twentieth century, look upon it, admiring its simple dignity and quiet beauty. While studying the picture, noting the perspective, color, and atmosphere, we are surprised that so beautiful an example of landscape art was possible two hundred years ago!

STUDY FOR APPRECIATION

1. How old is this picture?
   Is the painting "real" or "imaginative"?
   How does it differ from earlier landscape painting?

2. What do you think the most interesting feature of the picture. Why?
   What do you think the artist considered most interesting? Why?
   What is the setting for the "center of interest"?

3. What proportion of the canvas is sky? Land?

4. How does the light fall upon the scene?

What is the dominant tone of the painting?

Describe the cloud patterns.

What is their general direction?

Describe the appearance of the trees.

How are they spaced?

5. How has the artist repeated the vertical accents? Horizontal?

What gives repose and quiet to the picture?

6. Make a pencil sketch of the picture, massing in the setting, but emphasizing the "center of interest."

7. Who is the artist?

When did he live? Where?

8. When was his artistic ability recognized?

How does he rank today?

Related Music: SWEET REPOSE IS REIGNING NOW..
................*Benedict*

PRONUNCIATION OF PROPER NAMES

COPHETUA .... (cō fĕt′ ū ă)

COLLEONI, BARTOLOMMEO
.... (bär tŏl′ ō mā ō cŏl′ ē ō nĭ)

COROT, JEAN BAPTISTE
    CAMILLE.................
. (zhän băp′ tēest′ kă′ mēel′ kō′ rō′)

LOUVRE .... (lōō′ vr)

METCALF .... (mĕt′ kaf)

WATTS .... (wŏtz)

PETTIE .... (pĕt ĭ)

HOBBEMA, MEINDERT......
.... (mīn′ dĕrt hŏb′ ĕ ma)

TER BORCH .... (tĕr bôrk)

VERROCCHIO ..... (vĕr rō′ kē ō)

SUGGESTIONS TO TEACHERS

STUDYING THE PICTURE. Any picture presented for study becomes more interesting when freely discussed in a natural way by the class. Before reading the text it is always advisable to study the picture. Pupils should be encouraged to give their own impressions; tell what they like in a picture, and WHY they like it.

In the intermediate and grammar grades simple elements in picture making may be pointed out—*i. e.*, light and shade, repetition of line, of color, color harmony balance and center of interest. Such questions as,—From what direction does the light come? Where does it shine brightest? — and others of a similar nature, may help the pupil to SEE. Led by the teacher's skillful questioning, pupils gradually acquire the ability to discover for themselves many elements of design in picture-making.

DRAMATIZATION. Many of the pictures used in the intermediate and grammar grades lend themselves to dramatization. Under no circumstances is it necessary to burden oneself, in the class room, with an exact reproduction. The details of costume are not required. Any outstanding accessory of dress, easily at hand, may, however, add interest. It is the pose of the figure, the grouping if there are several, and the action, that are best appreciated by the pupils when the effort is made to reproduce a picture.

CORRELATION. Many of the famous pictures of this series bear directly upon interesting historical events. These, in particular, furnish subjects for language and composition.

Drawing lessons may with real profit be given over to the tracing of pictures, for the purpose of studying line, composition, light, and shade.

The music hour offers still another opportunity for related study. Pictures, like music, create emotions. When possible in the study of pictures, add the music which suggests the spirit and atmosphere of the picture. THE INTEREST IS ALWAYS KEENLY STIMULATED WHEN PORTIONS FROM VARIOUS SELECTIONS ARE PLAYED, AND THE CHILDREN PERMITTED TO CHOOSE THE ONE BEST SUITED TO THE PICTURE.

The suggestions for musical selections which follow the questions on the picture, will be of great value to the teacher.

As far as possible, each pupil should own his own pictures. This leads to the making of picture-study books, envelopes, and folders, for preserving his pictures.

STUDY OF ARTISTS. Many times when studying an artist, children are delighted to bring to the class room other reproductions of his pictures. This always stimulates interest. With several pictures by the same artist before the class, the outstanding characteristics of the painter, whether in color, composition, or some other phase of picture-making, may be intelligently discussed by the pupils. After such study as this, what "Millet" or "Rembrandt" will not be instantly recognized!

Sometimes bringing in pictures of the same subject by different artists is an equally interesting form of study. Such a series under a general subject,—as "Knighthood," "Trees," "Boats," "Joan of Arc,"—affords many opportunities for valuable comparisons. Children will readily discover that each of the artists, treating the same subject, tells his story in a different way. This cultivates intelligent SEEING, and appreciation.

Free discussion and pictures before the class are always vital to real enjoyment of the masterpieces.

To be introduced in early years to the masterpieces of the ages, and to learn of the kingly minds who have ruled in this realm of beauty, is sure to develop an interest which will enlarge, enrich, and refine the future life of the pupil.